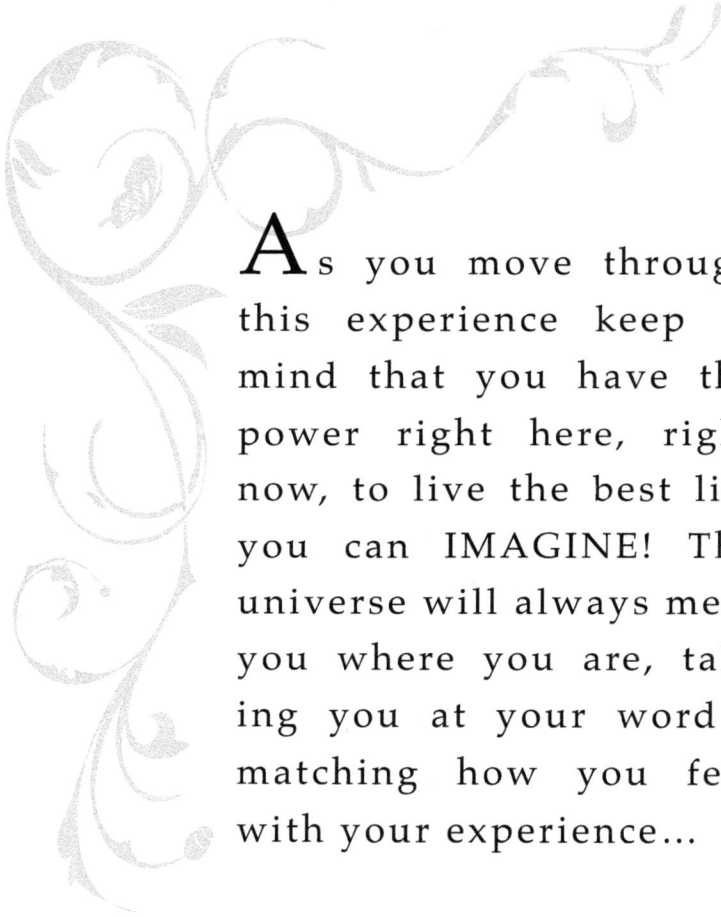

As you move through this experience keep in mind that you have the power right here, right now, to live the best life you can IMAGINE! The universe will always meet you where you are, taking you at your word... matching how you feel with your experience...

I am the Manifester

Play Book

by Tobi Ellison

The author and those associated with him shall not be liable or responsible for any damage or injury allegedly arising from the methods, formulas or information put forth in this book. This book is a self-help and inspirational guide for personal development. We assume no responsibility for inaccuracies or omissions.

No part of this book may be produced commercially either by off-set printing, digital printing or on the internet without permission of the publisher.

I Am The Manifester Play Book © 2013
by Tobi Ellison
an imprint of All About Manifesting

www.iamthemanifester.com

First Printing

ToBe Ellison Press

The world is perfect just
as it is... I will notice
this truth, when I stop
looking for things to
complain about...

Introduction

I have designed this book into two parts.

Morning Affirmation Treatment... the morning treatment is simple. Choose an affirmation from the book *I am the Manifester* or one from the playbook. The trick is choosing an affirmation that empowers you. One that evokes emotion and belief, so that when you say it you feel inspired to change. You will feel that the repetitive writing and speaking will bring great shifts into your life.

Evening Story-telling Treatment... Now that you know what you want, how will it FEEL to have the life you desire? How does it FEEL to have the money, lover, husband, new house, new car, better health, peace of mind, etc...? Now is the time to get into the FEELING space of your desire. You have heard the phrase act as if... allow yourself to be as a little child and dream... to tell a new story from that magical place of innocence.

Once you have chosen an area of life you wish to improve upon, move to the treatment process and decide what you most desire right now. You will have up to twelve weeks to manifest your desires. This must be done in a state of joy and excitement because you are becoming a conscious Manifester! Please feel free to revisit the book *I am the Manifester* and reread your favorite stories for inspiration. I tell you if a thirteen-year old can do it so can you! Now get to it and dream big!

*I awaken to new levels
of love undiscovered…*

WEEK 1

morning
Affirmation

_____
_____
_____
_____
_____
_____
_____
_____
_____
_____
_____
_____
_____
_____
_____
_____
_____
_____
_____
_____
_____
_____
_____
_____
_____
_____
_____

evening

Now that you are living this experience, how does it feel?

_____

_____

_____

_____

_____

_____

_____

_____

_____

_____

_____

_____

_____

_____

_____

_____

_____

_____

_____

_____

_____

_____

_____

morning
Affirmation

_____
_____
_____
_____
_____
_____
_____
_____
_____
_____
_____
_____
_____
_____
_____
_____
_____
_____
_____
_____
_____
_____
_____
_____
_____
_____
_____
_____

evening

Now that you are living this experience, how does it feel?

date: _____

morning
Affirmation

_____
_____
_____
_____
_____
_____
_____
_____
_____
_____
_____
_____
_____
_____
_____
_____
_____
_____
_____
_____
_____
_____
_____
_____
_____
_____
_____

evening

Now that you are living this experience, how does it feel?

morning Affirmation

_____

_____

_____

_____

_____

_____

_____

_____

_____

_____

_____

_____

_____

_____

_____

_____

_____

_____

_____

_____

_____

_____

_____

_____

_____

_____

_____

_____

_____

_____

evening

Now that you are living this experience, how does it feel?

date: _____

morning
Affirmation

_____
_____
_____
_____
_____
_____
_____
_____
_____
_____
_____
_____
_____
_____
_____
_____
_____
_____
_____
_____
_____
_____
_____
_____
_____
_____
_____
_____
_____

date: _____

evening

Now that you are living this experience, how does it feel?

morning
Affirmation

_____

_____

_____

_____

_____

_____

_____

_____

_____

_____

_____

_____

_____

_____

_____

_____

_____

_____

_____

_____

_____

_____

_____

_____

_____

_____

_____

_____

_____

_____

evening

Now that you are living this experience, how does it feel?

morning Affirmation

_____

_____

_____

_____

_____

_____

_____

_____

_____

_____

_____

_____

_____

_____

_____

_____

_____

_____

_____

_____

_____

_____

_____

_____

_____

_____

_____

_____

_____

evening

Now that you are living this experience, how does it feel?

The opinions of others
have no power when
I am comfortable
in my skin.

WEEK 2

morning
Affirmation

_____

_____

_____

_____

_____

_____

_____

_____

_____

_____

_____

_____

_____

_____

_____

_____

_____

_____

_____

_____

_____

_____

_____

_____

_____

_____

_____

_____

evening

Now that you are living this experience, how does it feel?

_____

_____

_____

_____

_____

_____

_____

_____

_____

_____

_____

_____

_____

_____

_____

_____

_____

_____

_____

_____

_____

_____

_____

_____

_____

morning
Affirmation

_____
_____
_____
_____
_____
_____
_____
_____
_____
_____
_____
_____
_____
_____
_____
_____
_____
_____
_____
_____
_____
_____
_____
_____
_____
_____
_____
_____
_____

evening

Now that you are living this experience, how does it feel?

_____

_____

_____

_____

_____

_____

_____

_____

_____

_____

_____

_____

_____

_____

_____

_____

_____

_____

_____

_____

_____

_____

_____

_____

_____

morning Affirmation

_____
_____
_____
_____
_____
_____
_____
_____
_____
_____
_____
_____
_____
_____
_____
_____
_____
_____
_____
_____
_____
_____
_____
_____
_____
_____
_____
_____
_____

evening

Now that you are living this experience, how does it feel?

morning
Affirmation

_____

_____

_____

_____

_____

_____

_____

_____

_____

_____

_____

_____

_____

_____

_____

_____

_____

_____

_____

_____

_____

_____

_____

_____

_____

_____

_____

_____

evening

Now that you are living this experience, how does it feel?

_____

_____

_____

_____

_____

_____

_____

_____

_____

_____

_____

_____

_____

_____

_____

_____

_____

_____

_____

_____

_____

_____

_____

_____

_____

date: _____

morning
Affirmation

_____
_____
_____
_____
_____
_____
_____
_____
_____
_____
_____
_____
_____
_____
_____
_____
_____
_____
_____
_____
_____
_____
_____
_____
_____
_____
_____
_____

evening

Now that you are living this experience, how does it feel?

_____

_____

_____

_____

_____

_____

_____

_____

_____

_____

_____

_____

_____

_____

_____

_____

_____

_____

_____

_____

_____

_____

_____

_____

_____

morning
Affirmation

_____
_____
_____
_____
_____
_____
_____
_____
_____
_____
_____
_____
_____
_____
_____
_____
_____
_____
_____
_____
_____
_____
_____
_____
_____
_____
_____
_____
_____
_____

evening

Now that you are living this experience, how does it feel?

date: _____

morning
Affirmation

_____
_____
_____
_____
_____
_____
_____
_____
_____
_____
_____
_____
_____
_____
_____
_____
_____
_____
_____
_____
_____
_____
_____
_____
_____
_____
_____

evening

Now that you are living this experience, how does it feel?

_____

_____

_____

_____

_____

_____

_____

_____

_____

_____

_____

_____

_____

_____

_____

_____

_____

_____

_____

_____

_____

_____

_____

_____

_____

I am filled with thoughts
of infinite possibilities...
When I no longer
concern myself with what
the world thinks of me...

WEEK 3

morning
Affirmation

_____

_____

_____

_____

_____

_____

_____

_____

_____

_____

_____

_____

_____

_____

_____

_____

_____

_____

_____

_____

_____

_____

_____

_____

_____

_____

_____

_____

evening

Now that you are living this experience, how does it feel?

morning Affirmation

_____
_____
_____
_____
_____
_____
_____
_____
_____
_____
_____
_____
_____
_____
_____
_____
_____
_____
_____
_____
_____
_____
_____
_____
_____
_____

evening

Now that you are living this experience, how does it feel?

date: _____

morning
Affirmation

evening

Now that you are living this experience, how does it feel?

morning
Affirmation

_____

_____

_____

_____

_____

_____

_____

_____

_____

_____

_____

_____

_____

_____

_____

_____

_____

_____

_____

_____

_____

_____

_____

_____

_____

_____

_____

_____

evening

Now that you are living this experience, how does it feel?

morning
Affirmation

_____

_____

_____

_____

_____

_____

_____

_____

_____

_____

_____

_____

_____

_____

_____

_____

_____

_____

_____

_____

_____

_____

_____

_____

_____

_____

_____

_____

evening

Now that you are living this experience, how does it feel?

morning
Affirmation

_____
_____
_____
_____
_____
_____
_____
_____
_____
_____
_____
_____
_____
_____
_____
_____
_____
_____
_____
_____
_____
_____
_____
_____
_____
_____
_____
_____

evening

Now that you are living this experience, how does it feel?

date: _____

morning
Affirmation

_____
_____
_____
_____
_____
_____
_____
_____
_____
_____
_____
_____
_____
_____
_____
_____
_____
_____
_____
_____
_____
_____
_____
_____
_____
_____
_____
_____

date: _____

evening

Now that you are living this experience, how does it feel?

_____
_____
_____
_____
_____
_____
_____
_____
_____
_____
_____
_____
_____
_____
_____
_____
_____
_____
_____
_____
_____
_____
_____
_____
_____

There is nothing special about being special. It is the awareness of this truth that one becomes magnificent.

WEEK 4

morning
Affirmation

_____
_____
_____
_____
_____
_____
_____
_____
_____
_____
_____
_____
_____
_____
_____
_____
_____
_____
_____
_____
_____
_____
_____
_____
_____
_____
_____

evening

Now that you are living this experience, how does it feel?

date: _____

morning
Affirmation

_____
_____
_____
_____
_____
_____
_____
_____
_____
_____
_____
_____
_____
_____
_____
_____
_____
_____
_____
_____
_____
_____
_____
_____
_____
_____
_____
_____
_____
_____

evening

Now that you are living this experience, how does it feel?

morning
Affirmation

_____

_____

_____

_____

_____

_____

_____

_____

_____

_____

_____

_____

_____

_____

_____

_____

_____

_____

_____

_____

_____

_____

_____

_____

_____

_____

evening

Now that you are living this experience, how does it feel?

_____

_____

_____

_____

_____

_____

_____

_____

_____

_____

_____

_____

_____

_____

_____

_____

_____

_____

_____

_____

_____

_____

_____

_____

morning
Affirmation

evening

Now that you are living this experience, how does it feel?

_____

_____

_____

_____

_____

_____

_____

_____

_____

_____

_____

_____

_____

_____

_____

_____

_____

_____

_____

_____

_____

_____

_____

date: _____

morning
Affirmation

_____
_____
_____
_____
_____
_____
_____
_____
_____
_____
_____
_____
_____
_____
_____
_____
_____
_____
_____
_____
_____
_____
_____
_____
_____
_____
_____

evening

Now that you are living this experience, how does it feel?

morning
Affirmation

evening

Now that you are living this experience, how does it feel?

_____

_____

_____

_____

_____

_____

_____

_____

_____

_____

_____

_____

_____

_____

_____

_____

_____

_____

_____

_____

_____

_____

_____

_____

date: _____

morning
Affirmation

_____
_____
_____
_____
_____
_____
_____
_____
_____
_____
_____
_____
_____
_____
_____
_____
_____
_____
_____
_____
_____
_____
_____
_____
_____
_____
_____

evening

Now that you are living this experience, how does it feel?

_____

_____

_____

_____

_____

_____

_____

_____

_____

_____

_____

_____

_____

_____

_____

_____

_____

_____

_____

_____

_____

_____

_____

The misunderstanding
of who we are, leads
to fear and a desire to
judge... we then become
less than ourselves pro-
jecting our insecurities.

WEEK 5

morning
Affirmation

_____
_____
_____
_____
_____
_____
_____
_____
_____
_____
_____
_____
_____
_____
_____
_____
_____
_____
_____
_____
_____
_____
_____
_____
_____
_____
_____
_____

evening

Now that you are living this experience, how does it feel?

morning
Affirmation

_____

_____

_____

_____

_____

_____

_____

_____

_____

_____

_____

_____

_____

_____

_____

_____

_____

_____

_____

_____

_____

_____

_____

_____

_____

_____

_____

_____

_____

evening

Now that you are living this experience, how does it feel?

date: _____

morning
Affirmation

evening

Now that you are living this experience, how does it feel?

morning
Affirmation

evening

Now that you are living this experience, how does it feel?

morning
Affirmation

_____

_____

_____

_____

_____

_____

_____

_____

_____

_____

_____

_____

_____

_____

_____

_____

_____

_____

_____

_____

_____

_____

_____

_____

_____

_____

_____

_____

evening

Now that you are living this experience, how does it feel?

morning
Affirmation

_____

_____

_____

_____

_____

_____

_____

_____

_____

_____

_____

_____

_____

_____

_____

_____

_____

_____

_____

_____

_____

_____

_____

_____

_____

_____

_____

evening

Now that you are living this experience, how does it feel?

morning
Affirmation

_____
_____
_____
_____
_____
_____
_____
_____
_____
_____
_____
_____
_____
_____
_____
_____
_____
_____
_____
_____
_____
_____
_____
_____
_____
_____
_____
_____

evening

Now that you are living this experience, how does it feel?

Love feels wonderful,
as it flows through me,
reminding me of my
deepest truth. I know
life shall be
a reflection of
self-discovery...

WEEK 6

date: _____

morning
Affirmation

_____
_____
_____
_____
_____
_____
_____
_____
_____
_____
_____
_____
_____
_____
_____
_____
_____
_____
_____
_____
_____
_____
_____
_____
_____
_____
_____
_____

evening

Now that you are living this experience, how does it feel?

_____

_____

_____

_____

_____

_____

_____

_____

_____

_____

_____

_____

_____

_____

_____

_____

_____

_____

_____

_____

_____

morning
Affirmation

_____
_____
_____
_____
_____
_____
_____
_____
_____
_____
_____
_____
_____
_____
_____
_____
_____
_____
_____
_____
_____
_____
_____
_____
_____
_____
_____
_____

evening

Now that you are living this experience, how does it feel?

morning Affirmation

evening

Now that you are living this experience, how does it feel?

_____

_____

_____

_____

_____

_____

_____

_____

_____

_____

_____

_____

_____

_____

_____

_____

_____

_____

_____

_____

_____

_____

morning
Affirmation

_____

_____

_____

_____

_____

_____

_____

_____

_____

_____

_____

_____

_____

_____

_____

_____

_____

_____

_____

_____

_____

_____

_____

_____

_____

_____

_____

evening

Now that you are living this experience, how does it feel?

morning
Affirmation

_____
_____
_____
_____
_____
_____
_____
_____
_____
_____
_____
_____
_____
_____
_____
_____
_____
_____
_____
_____
_____
_____
_____
_____
_____
_____
_____
_____

evening

Now that you are living this experience, how does it feel?

_____

_____

_____

_____

_____

_____

_____

_____

_____

_____

_____

_____

_____

_____

_____

_____

_____

_____

_____

_____

_____

_____

date: _____

morning
Affirmation

_____
_____
_____
_____
_____
_____
_____
_____
_____
_____
_____
_____
_____
_____
_____
_____
_____
_____
_____
_____
_____
_____
_____
_____
_____
_____
_____
_____

evening

Now that you are living this experience, how does it feel?

_____

_____

_____

_____

_____

_____

_____

_____

_____

_____

_____

_____

_____

_____

_____

_____

_____

_____

_____

_____

_____

_____

_____

_____

_____

date: _____

morning
Affirmation

_____
_____
_____
_____
_____
_____
_____
_____
_____
_____
_____
_____
_____
_____
_____
_____
_____
_____
_____
_____
_____
_____
_____
_____
_____

evening

Now that you are living this experience, how does it feel?

Fear is an illusion
concocted by insecurity.

WEEK 7

date: _____

morning
Affirmation

date: _____

evening
Now that you are living this experience, how does it feel?

date: _____

morning
Affirmation

_____
_____
_____
_____
_____
_____
_____
_____
_____
_____
_____
_____
_____
_____
_____
_____
_____
_____
_____
_____
_____
_____
_____
_____
_____
_____
_____

evening

Now that you are living this experience, how does it feel?

date: _____

morning
Affirmation

---

evening

Now that you are living this experience, how does it feel?

morning
Affirmation

_____
_____
_____
_____
_____
_____
_____
_____
_____
_____
_____
_____
_____
_____
_____
_____
_____
_____
_____
_____
_____
_____
_____
_____
_____
_____
_____
_____

evening

Now that you are living this experience, how does it feel?

date: _____

morning
Affirmation

evening

Now that you are living this experience, how does it feel?

morning
Affirmation

_____
_____
_____
_____
_____
_____
_____
_____
_____
_____
_____
_____
_____
_____
_____
_____
_____
_____
_____
_____
_____
_____
_____
_____
_____
_____

evening

Now that you are living this experience, how does it feel?

morning
Affirmation

_____
_____
_____
_____
_____
_____
_____
_____
_____
_____
_____
_____
_____
_____
_____
_____
_____
_____
_____
_____
_____
_____
_____
_____
_____
_____
_____
_____

evening

Now that you are living this experience, how does it feel?

_____
_____
_____
_____
_____
_____
_____
_____
_____
_____
_____
_____
_____
_____
_____
_____
_____
_____
_____
_____
_____
_____
_____
_____
_____
_____

I now realize I must save myself, I understand no one can save me, nor can I save them… we are perfect just as we are…
PURE LOVE!

WEEK 8

date: _____

morning
Affirmation

_____
_____
_____
_____
_____
_____
_____
_____
_____
_____
_____
_____
_____
_____
_____
_____
_____
_____
_____
_____
_____
_____
_____
_____
_____
_____
_____
_____
_____
_____

evening

Now that you are living this experience, how does it feel?

date: _____

morning
Affirmation

_____
_____
_____
_____
_____
_____
_____
_____
_____
_____
_____
_____
_____
_____
_____
_____
_____
_____
_____
_____
_____
_____
_____
_____
_____
_____
_____

evening

Now that you are living this experience, how does it feel?

_____
_____
_____
_____
_____
_____
_____
_____
_____
_____
_____
_____
_____
_____
_____
_____
_____
_____
_____
_____
_____
_____
_____

morning
Affirmation

_____

_____

_____

_____

_____

_____

_____

_____

_____

_____

_____

_____

_____

_____

_____

_____

_____

_____

_____

_____

_____

_____

_____

_____

_____

_____

evening

Now that you are living this experience, how does it feel?

morning
Affirmation

_____
_____
_____
_____
_____
_____
_____
_____
_____
_____
_____
_____
_____
_____
_____
_____
_____
_____
_____
_____
_____
_____
_____
_____
_____
_____

evening

Now that you are living this experience, how does it feel?

morning
Affirmation

evening

Now that you are living this experience, how does it feel?

_____

_____

_____

_____

_____

_____

_____

_____

_____

_____

_____

_____

_____

_____

_____

_____

_____

_____

_____

_____

_____

_____

_____

_____

_____

morning Affirmation

evening

Now that you are living this experience, how does it feel?

morning
Affirmation

_____
_____
_____
_____
_____
_____
_____
_____
_____
_____
_____
_____
_____
_____
_____
_____
_____
_____
_____
_____
_____
_____
_____
_____
_____
_____

evening

Now that you are living this experience, how does it feel?

The Universe is the perfect matchmaker; it brings me all I am choosing to think about...I am now choosing to be a conscious manifester.

WEEK 9

date: _____

morning
Affirmation

_____
_____
_____
_____
_____
_____
_____
_____
_____
_____
_____
_____
_____
_____
_____
_____
_____
_____
_____
_____
_____
_____
_____
_____
_____
_____
_____

evening

Now that you are living this experience, how does it feel?

date: _____

morning
Affirmation

_____
_____
_____
_____
_____
_____
_____
_____
_____
_____
_____
_____
_____
_____
_____
_____
_____
_____
_____
_____
_____
_____
_____
_____
_____
_____
_____

evening

Now that you are living this experience, how does it feel?

date: _____

morning
Affirmation

evening

Now that you are living this experience, how does it feel?

morning Affirmation

_____
_____
_____
_____
_____
_____
_____
_____
_____
_____
_____
_____
_____
_____
_____
_____
_____
_____
_____
_____
_____
_____
_____
_____
_____
_____
_____

evening

Now that you are living this experience, how does it feel?

date: _____

morning
Affirmation

_____
_____
_____
_____
_____
_____
_____
_____
_____
_____
_____
_____
_____
_____
_____
_____
_____
_____
_____
_____
_____
_____
_____
_____
_____
_____
_____

evening

Now that you are living this experience, how does it feel?

morning
Affirmation

_____
_____
_____
_____
_____
_____
_____
_____
_____
_____
_____
_____
_____
_____
_____
_____
_____
_____
_____
_____
_____
_____
_____
_____
_____
_____
_____

evening

Now that you are living this experience, how does it feel?

_____
_____
_____
_____
_____
_____
_____
_____
_____
_____
_____
_____
_____
_____
_____
_____
_____
_____
_____
_____
_____
_____
_____
_____
_____

morning Affirmation

evening

Now that you are living this experience, how does it feel?

When I am in a state of appreciation, I find inspiration in every moment, in everyone and everything.

WEEK 10

date: _____

morning
Affirmation

_____
_____
_____
_____
_____
_____
_____
_____
_____
_____
_____
_____
_____
_____
_____
_____
_____
_____
_____
_____
_____
_____
_____
_____
_____
_____
_____

evening

Now that you are living this experience, how does it feel?

morning Affirmation

evening

Now that you are living this experience, how does it feel?

_____

_____

_____

_____

_____

_____

_____

_____

_____

_____

_____

_____

_____

_____

_____

_____

_____

_____

_____

_____

_____

_____

_____

date: _____

morning Affirmation

evening

Now that you are living this experience, how does it feel?

morning
Affirmation

_____

_____

_____

_____

_____

_____

_____

_____

_____

_____

_____

_____

_____

_____

_____

_____

_____

_____

_____

_____

_____

_____

_____

_____

_____

_____

_____

_____

date: _____

evening

Now that you are living this experience, how does it feel?

date: _____

morning
Affirmation

_____
_____
_____
_____
_____
_____
_____
_____
_____
_____
_____
_____
_____
_____
_____
_____
_____
_____
_____
_____
_____
_____
_____
_____
_____
_____

evening

Now that you are living this experience, how does it feel?

date: _____

morning
Affirmation

_____
_____
_____
_____
_____
_____
_____
_____
_____
_____
_____
_____
_____
_____
_____
_____
_____
_____
_____
_____
_____
_____
_____
_____
_____

evening

Now that you are living this experience, how does it feel?

morning
Affirmation

evening

Now that you are living this experience, how does it feel?

When I have given
enough thought to my
desires the universe gives
me clues... signs if you
will, as to what I
should do next.

WEEK 11

date: _____

morning
Affirmation

evening

Now that you are living this experience, how does it feel?

date: _____

morning Affirmation

date: _____

evening

Now that you are living this
experience, how does it feel?

date: _____

morning
Affirmation

_____
_____
_____
_____
_____
_____
_____
_____
_____
_____
_____
_____
_____
_____
_____
_____
_____
_____
_____
_____
_____
_____
_____
_____
_____
_____
_____

evening

Now that you are living this experience, how does it feel?

morning
Affirmation

_____
_____
_____
_____
_____
_____
_____
_____
_____
_____
_____
_____
_____
_____
_____
_____
_____
_____
_____
_____
_____
_____
_____
_____
_____

evening

Now that you are living this experience, how does it feel?

date: _____

morning
Affirmation

_____
_____
_____
_____
_____
_____
_____
_____
_____
_____
_____
_____
_____
_____
_____
_____
_____
_____
_____
_____
_____
_____
_____
_____
_____
_____
_____
_____

evening

Now that you are living this experience, how does it feel?

date: _____

morning
Affirmation

_____
_____
_____
_____
_____
_____
_____
_____
_____
_____
_____
_____
_____
_____
_____
_____
_____
_____
_____
_____
_____
_____
_____
_____
_____
_____
_____

evening

Now that you are living this experience, how does it feel?

date: _____

morning
Affirmation

evening

Now that you are living this experience, how does it feel?

The judgments made
against my brother are
but reflections of my own
shortcomings.

WEEK 12

morning
Affirmation

_____
_____
_____
_____
_____
_____
_____
_____
_____
_____
_____
_____
_____
_____
_____
_____
_____
_____
_____
_____
_____
_____
_____
_____
_____
_____

evening

Now that you are living this experience, how does it feel?

morning
Affirmation

_____

_____

_____

_____

_____

_____

_____

_____

_____

_____

_____

_____

_____

_____

_____

_____

_____

_____

_____

_____

_____

_____

_____

_____

_____

_____

evening

Now that you are living this experience, how does it feel?

morning Affirmation

date: _____

evening

Now that you are living this experience, how does it feel?

date: _____

morning
Affirmation

_____
_____
_____
_____
_____
_____
_____
_____
_____
_____
_____
_____
_____
_____
_____
_____
_____
_____
_____
_____
_____
_____
_____
_____
_____
_____
_____
_____
_____

evening

Now that you are living this experience, how does it feel?

morning
Affirmation

evening

Now that you are living this experience, how does it feel?

date: _____

morning
Affirmation

evening

Now that you are living this experience, how does it feel?

date: _____

morning
Affirmation

evening

Now that you are living this experience, how does it feel?

_____

_____

_____

_____

_____

_____

_____

_____

_____

_____

_____

_____

_____

_____

_____

_____

_____

_____

_____

_____

_____

_____

_____

_____

_____

Affirmations for Manifesting

Well being
AFFIRMATIONS

*I am experiencing well- being... as I allow things
to flow in my life, just as they are.*

*I am well-being... In every breath,
I am reminded of this truth.*

*I am inspired to well-being in my thoughts,
words and deeds.*

*I am well-being, just as I am and
the world responds accordingly.*

*I am in a state of well-being and
all is right in my world.*

Love
AFFIRMATIONS

*In every moment, I am making a
conscious choice to choose love.*

*I am pure love, true love, without conditions...
I give love freely.*

I am love and it's my constant companion

*I am loving life fully, being filled with all I am
giving... flowing freely... my cup runneth over.*

*I am the love I seek made manifest
as my lover, husband, wife, friend.*

*I am lovingly embracing every aspect I see... and for
this, I am pleased with the face staring back at me.*

Peace

AFFIRMATIONS

I am at peace with my world and all is peaceful.

*I am a peaceful person and therefore I attract
peaceful people in all my affairs...*

*With every perceived problem comes
a peaceful solution.*

I am meeting more peaceful people on a daily basis.

I am working in a peaceful environment.

I am in a peaceful relationship.

Joy
AFFIRMATIONS

In every moment, I am choosing to be joyous.

I am filled with joy, in my mind body and soul.

It's a joy being... who I am, just as I am.

I am open to feeling more joy, being more joyful.

*I am experiencing more joy in
every way of every day.*

*It's a joy to just be... I like the person I see... and all
I'm meant to be is right here, inside of me...*

Money
AFFIRMATIONS

I am a money magnet, money flows and
grows in all my affairs.

I am tuned into the magic of money...
flowing into my life under grace.

I have more money to spend and even more money
to lend to my family and friends.

I am open to money coming to me
in miraculous ways.

I am the energy of money flowing out into the
world... and back into my accounts...
all in large amounts.

I give money, freely and money returns easily,
effortlessly and daily.

Abundance

AFFIRMATIONS

I am abundance filled with more then enough to give.

I am living abundantly, giving the best of me...

I am abundant in every aspect of my life...
appreciating all I have and all that is...

I am feeling more abundant in every moment in
every breath, I am reminded of the
abundance in the world.

I am in the flow of grace living my best life....
I am in abundance right here, right now... I am it.